A New True Book

THE NAVAJO

By Alice Osinski

Consultant: Robert Bell, Ph.D.
University of New Mexico

CHILDRENS PRESS ®
CHICAGO

At the Little Colorado River Gorge, south of the Grand Canyon

For Mary Baldwin

Library of Congress Cataloging-in-Publication Data

Osinski, Alice.
   The Navajo.

   (A New true book)
   Includes index.
   Summary: A brief history of the Navajo Indians describing customs, interactions with white settlers, and changes in traditional ways of life brought on by modern civilization.
   1. Navajo Indians—Juvenile literature.
[1. Navajo Indians. 2. Indians of North America]
I. Title.
E99.N30A5 1987   973'.0497   86-30978
ISBN 0-516-01236-3

FIFTH PRINTING 1992 Childrens Press®, Chicago
Copyright © 1987 by Regensteiner Publishing Enterprises, Inc.
All rights reserved. Published simultaneously in Canada.
Printed in the United States of America.
    7 8 9 10 R 00 99 98 97 96 95 94

PHOTO CREDITS
© Reinhard Brucker—10 (left), 29 (top left), 33, 35 (right), 37
© Cameramann International, Ltd.—11, 27 (left), 41 (2 photos), 42 (3 photos)
The Collected Image, Odyssey Productions, Chicago—17
© Joan Dunlop—Cover, 27 (right), 29 (middle left), 43 (left)
Museum of the American Indian—29 (middle right)
Nawrocki Stock Photo: © Jeff Apoian—30 (bottom left)
© Photo Source International—14, 31, 45
© Photri—4 (top), 7 (bottom), 8 (left), 9 (right), 30 (top left)
© H. Armstrong Roberts—25
Root Resources:
© James Blank—8
© Pat Monsarratt—39
© L. Munson—13
© John Running Photographs—4 (bottom), 7 (top), 9 (left), 10 (right), 15, 29 (bottom left and top right), 30 (bottom right and top right), 35 (left), 38 (2 photos), 40 (2 photos)
Smithsonian Institution, Bureau of American Ethnology Collection—23 (2 photos)
Tom Stack & Associates:
© David Burckhalter—44
© Brian Parker—43 (right)
Western History Collections, University of Oklahoma Library—26
© Jerome Wyckoff—2
Odyssey Productions, Chicago: © Robert Frerck—29 (bottom right)
Courtesy Museum of New Mexico—18 (Neg. No. 38207), 21 (right; Neg. No. 1816)
Courtesy of Arizona Historical Society, Tucson—21 (left)
Cover: Bruce and Bernice Jackson

TABLE OF CONTENTS

Diné—The People...5

Earth Houses...10

The Spanish Bring Sheep...12

The Long Walk...17

Fort Sumner...22

Reservation Life...25

Silver and Wool...27

The Holy People...32

Modern Ways...38

Words You Should Know...46

Index...48

DINÉ: THE PEOPLE

In a dry, rocky area of Arizona, a pick-up truck races along a paved highway. Nearby a shepherd walks his flock of sheep along a dirt road. Both old and modern ways of life exist side-by-side among the Navajo, the largest tribe of North American Indians.

Navajos, or *Diné* as they call themselves, live on

Navajo land surrounds the
small area of land the Hopi Indians
live on in Arizona.

more than 25,000 square
miles of land. This land
stretches across parts of
Arizona, Utah, and New
Mexico.

A long time ago
ancestors of the Navajo
lived in northwestern
Canada and Alaska. About

Navajos look out over the beauty surrounding them:
San Francisco Mountains (above)
and Monument Valley, Utah (below).

Remains of Pueblo Bonito, a 4-story, 800-room apartment dwelling in Chaco Canyon, New Mexico. The dwelling was built by Pueblos and later occupied by Navajos.

1,000 years ago they began traveling south. When they reached southwestern United States they met people who had been farming there for many centuries. Today, these people are known as Pueblo Indians.

Corn played an important part in Navajo life. Men raised it. Women ground it into flour for bread.

The Navajos settled near the Pueblos and learned many things from them. They learned how to plant corn, beans, squash, and melons. In time, Navajo styles of clothing, weaving, and pottery became similar to Pueblo styles.

EARTH HOUSES

Navajos made their
homes, called *hogans*, of
wooden poles, tree bark,
and mud. They built them
with four support poles.
The doorway of each
hogan opened to the east
so Navajos could welcome

the morning sun and
receive good blessings.
Today, many Navajo
families still live in hogans.
They build the four-sided
hogan or the older form
which is round and cone-
shaped.

THE SPANISH BRING SHEEP

In the 1600s when the Spanish settled in the Southwest, Navajo life changed. The Spanish brought sheep and horses with them from Europe. When Navajos began stealing the sheep and horses, they learned how to use them in their daily life.

From sheep's wool, they

Herding sheep in Monument Valley

wove clothing, blankets,
and rugs. Sheep also
provided meat for food.
In time the sheep herd
became very important.
Navajo families began to
center their lives around the
needs of the herd. Soon

Horses are still an important means of transportation for Navajos.
There are few paved roads through their dry, rocky land.

more respect was given
to families who had larger
herds that were well cared for.
  Horses were very
important to the Navajo, too.
With the aid of horses

A rock painting in Canyon de Chelly in Arizona shows the arrival of the Spaniards on horses.

they could travel longer distances on raiding parties. They could trade more. Although the Navajos liked the sheep and horses that the Spanish brought, they did

15

not like many of the
Spanish customs.

Spanish soldiers fought
the Native Americans. They
made prisoners of them
and used them as servants.
At different times the Navajo,
Pueblo, and Apache joined
together to fight off the
Spanish. The Pueblo only
won briefly, but the Navajo
and Apache remained free.
They continued to fight
and raid the Spanish.

This photograph of Canyon de Chelly was taken by Edward Curtis in the early 1900s. He devoted his life to photographing Native Americans.

THE LONG WALK

During the 1800s, the United States acquired land from Mexico, which later became the states of Arizona and New Mexico. When settlers, looking

Many fine studio portraits were taken of Navajos from the 1800s until about 1910.

for silver and gold, came into the area where the Navajo lived, fighting broke out. As the Navajo fought to keep their land, the settlers fought to take it away.

Many written agreements, called treaties, were made

between the United States government and Navajo leaders. But neither side could make their people keep the agreements. Over the years many events caused bad feelings between the Navajo and the settlers. Land was stolen and people were killed.

In 1849 Narbona, an important Navajo leader, was shot by American soldiers. Then in 1860

Navajos attacked
Fort Defiance in Arizona.
The United States decided
to stop the Navajo.
Between 1864 and 1865
U.S. troops, led by
Christopher (Kit) Carson,
forced more than 8,000
Navajos off their land.
They were made prisoners
and were forced to walk

Fort Defiance

Navajo prisoners construct a
building at Fort Sumner.

more than 300 miles across
New Mexico to Fort Sumner.
Before reaching the fort
more than 300 Navajos
died. This forced march
is called the Long Walk.

FORT SUMNER

Life was terrible at Fort Sumner in New Mexico. The Navajo were homesick for their land. They were brokenhearted. Disease and starvation caused more than 2,000 of them to die. After four years the U.S. government saw that their plan to make Navajos live like whites had failed. They made a new treaty with the Navajo.

Narbona Primero (left) was photographed around 1874.
This photograph of Barboncito (right) was taken around 1870.

Barboncito and nineteen
other Navajo leaders
signed the new treaty in
1868. Afterwards, the
Navajos were free to

return to their country. But
Navajos could return only
to the area called the "Treaty
Reservation." This section
of land was surrounded by
non-Indians who had
moved onto the land while
the Navajo had been
away. They had built
towns around early trading
posts. In the future the
Santa Fe Railroad would
be bringing more people
into this area.

RESERVATION LIFE

When Navajos returned
from Fort Sumner, they began
building homes and planting
gardens and orchards. Once
again herds of sheep were
grazing on the land. But
reservation life changed
many things. Children were

A school baseball team

taken away from their families
and sent to boarding schools.
They learned to dress, speak,
and act as non-Indian
children did. Contact with
nearby towns brought more
change. Navajos sometimes
found it hard to be both
Navajo and American.

SILVER AND WOOL

In order to make money, Navajos began making items they could trade in town. Soon trading posts were built on the reservation to sell their fine, handmade crafts. Tourists came to buy them.

Navajo crafts are sold at Hubbell's historic trading post near Ganado, Arizona (left) and the Goulding's trading post (right).

Today, Navajo women still weave colorful belts, rugs, and blankets from homespun wool. They sit on sheepskin wool on the ground in front of a large wooden loom. Some still use natural vegetable dyes to create the red, blue, and green colors that their grandmothers used long before them.

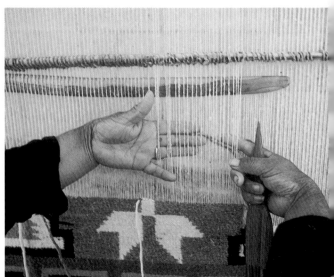

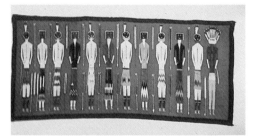

Women weave colorful blankets on their looms. There are three basic types of Navajo weaving—regular weaves, double weaves, and two-faced weaves.

Navajos take pride in their
silversmithing. Their love of
beauty shows in the finely
crafted jewelry they wear.
Some of the best examples
of old Navajo silver can
be found in museums and
collections off the reservation.

Navajo artists are known for their silverwork, which they learned from some Mexican people. Silver decorated with a blue stone called turquoise is cut to make beautiful bracelets, rings, earrings, belts, and necklaces.

THE HOLY PEOPLE

Singing has special meaning for Navajos. Each song or chant is a prayer to the Holy People or supernatural beings whom the Navajo believe watch over life. Some of these beings are Talking God, Changing Woman, Bear, Ant, and Corn People.

Navajo songs are sung

Navajo woodcarving of the Eagle Dance

in ceremonies to cure the
sick or to protect their
families, homes, crops, and
herds. One of the more
important Navajo
ceremonies is called
"Blessingway." It is

not for curing. Instead,
it provides a blessing for
a long and happy life.
Also, it is used to bless
a new hogan or a new
marriage. Every Navajo
ceremony or "sing" includes
a Blessingway song.

A special person called
a "singer" or "Medicine
Man" learns the songs for
each ceremony. Before
beginning each ceremony
the Medicine Man or
Woman makes a

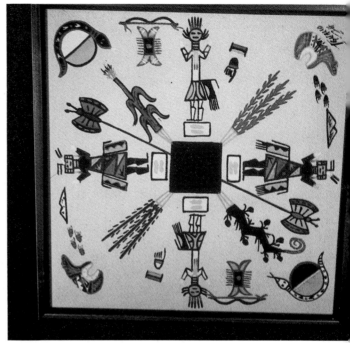

A medicine man (left).
The sandpainting "Home of the
Bear and the Snake" (right)

sandpainting on the floor
of the hogan. He or she
carefully sprinkles colored
vegetable or mineral
powders on a layer of
sand in the forms of the

35

Holy People who will be helping to cure or protect the person being sung over. Sometimes the Holy People are painted in pairs, standing on rainbows, their means of transportation.

After the sandpainting is completed, the singing begins. Sometime during the ceremony, the sick person sits on the painting

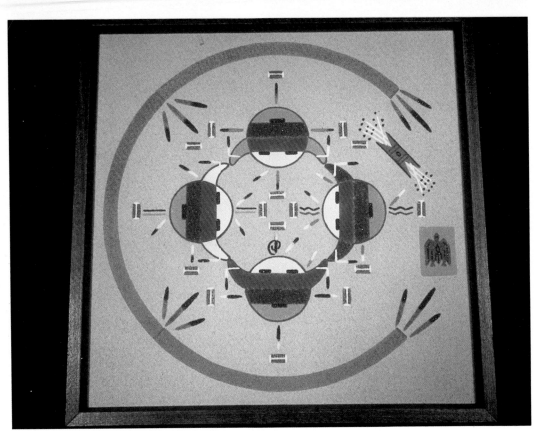

"Four Houses of the Sun" is a sandpainting used for healing.

to receive power from the
Holy People. When the
ceremony is over, the painting
is rubbed away. Then the
sand is carried outside to
the North and left there.

MODERN WAYS

For most Navajos, life is very different from the quiet life their grandfathers knew. Although many Navajos follow the old ways as closely as they

A woman carding sheep's wool. The wool must be free from knots before it can be spun. Then it is ready to be woven.

can, modern life makes it very difficult.

As some Navajo women sit quietly weaving at their looms, others on the reservation are operating huge drills that take gas and oil from the ground.

While some Navajo men work hard to bring water to their hogans, workmen nearby are hauling away large parts of land in search of coal. These gas, oil, coal, and power companies are changing the countryside and causing problems for Navajos.

Navajo power plant (left) near Page, Arizona and the
Navajo Council Chamber (right) at Window Rock, Arizona.

It is the job of the
Navajo Tribal Council to
take care of the problems
on the reservation. The
council makes sure that
the land is protected. It also
tries hard to create jobs
and provide good

The Navajo depend on three important sources to make their life better: education at the Navajo Community College (right), federal assistance funds for modern communities (bottom left), and the tourist trade (bottom right).

education and health care for the tribe. The Navajo Community College helps solve problems, too. It

prepares many people to
become teachers, nurses,
lawyers, and engineers.

Someday, they in turn will make life better for Navajos.

About 1977, the Navajo opened an office in Washington, D.C., close to the Congress of the United States. Since then they

have been fighting for the
rights of all Native
Americans. They have
been reminding leaders
in Washington to use
land wisely and care
for the people who live
and depend on it.

WORDS YOU SHOULD KNOW

ancestor(AN • sess • ter) — a family member from whom you have descended

Apache(ah • PAT • chee) — a tribe of North American Indians of New Mexico and Southwestern United States

boarding school(BORD • ing SKOOL) — a school, away from home, where children are provided with meals and lodging during the school terms

Barboncito(bar • bon • SEE • toh) — a Navajo Indian leader who with nineteen other Navajo leaders signed a new treaty with the United States in 1868 allowing the tribe to return to their land in Arizona and New Mexico

Blessingway(BLESS • ing • way) — a Navajo ceremony blessing a marriage, a home, a long happy life, crops, and other ventures

Kit Carson(KIT CAR • sun) — an early frontiersman, guide, and Indian fighter who led United States troops in forcing more than 8,000 Navajos off their land

century(SEN • shur • ee) — a one-hundred-year period

ceremony(SAIR • ih • moh • nee) — a special celebration or ritual for a notable occasion

Congress(KAHN • gress) — the assembled United States senators and representatives

cornmeal(KORN • meel) — coarsely ground corn kernels used in making bread

Diné(DEE • nay) — Navajo Indian word meaning people

hogan(HO • gun) — an earth-covered house of the Navajo Indian

homespun(HOAM • spun) — coarse cloth, blankets, rugs and the like made from wool yarn spun and woven in the home

Holy People(HOLE • ee PEEP • il) — supernatural beings whom the Navajo Indians believe watch over life

Hopi(HOPE • ee) — a North American Indian tribe of northeastern Arizona